The Alphabet Is Missing

Level 4+
Blue+

Helpful Hints for Reading at Home

The graphemes (written letters) and phonemes (units of sound) used throughout this series are aligned with Letters and Sounds. This offers a consistent approach to learning whether reading at home or in the classroom.

THIS BLUE+ BOOK BAND SERVES AS AN INTRODUCTION TO PHASE 5. EACH BOOK IN THIS BAND USES ALL PHONEMES LEARNED UP TO PHASE 4, WHILE INTRODUCING ONE PHASE 5 PHONEME. HERE IS A LIST OF PHONEMES FOR THIS PHASE, WITH THE NEW PHASE 5 PHONEME. AN EXAMPLE OF THE PRONUNCIATION CAN BE FOUND IN BRACKETS.

Phase 3			
j (jug)	v (van)	w (wet)	x (fox)
y (yellow)	z (zoo)	zz (buzz)	qu (quick)
ch (chip)	sh (shop)	th (thin/then)	ng (ring)
ai (rain)	ee (feet)	igh (night)	oa (boat)
oo (boot/look)	ar (farm)	or (for)	ur (hurt)
ow (cow)	oi (coin)	ear (dear)	air (fair)
ure (sure)	er (corner)		

New Phase 5 Phoneme	ph (alphabet, phantom)

HERE ARE SOME WORDS WHICH YOUR CHILD MAY FIND TRICKY.

Phase 4 Tricky Words			
said	were	have	there
like	little	so	one
do	when	some	out
come	what		

TOP TIPS FOR HELPING YOUR CHILD TO READ:

- Allow children time to break down unfamiliar words into units of sound and then encourage children to string these sounds together to create the word.

- Encourage your child to point out any focus phonics when they are used.

- Read through the book more than once to grow confidence.

- Ask simple questions about the text to assess understanding.

- Encourage children to use illustrations as prompts.

This book introduces the phoneme /ph/ and is a Blue+ Level 4+ book band.

The Alphabet Is Missing

Written by Madeline Tyler

Illustrated by Richard Bayley

"Ralph!" yells Delph. "You need to return that book to the book club in town!"

"I lost it!" yells Ralph. "It was on my bed but now it is not there!"

Delph sighs. She runs up the stairs to help Ralph look for his book.

They look under his coat and on his desk, but the book is not there.

Delph spots a card on Ralph's bed. It has a dolphin on it.

"Some of the alphabet is missing! Look!" Delph tells Ralph as she points at the card.

Letters of the alphabet crash and zoom across the room.

"We need to track down the alphabet. Grab that bag," Delph tells Ralph.

The alphabet letters go down the road. Delph and Ralph run, but the letters are too quick!

"We need some oomph," groans Ralph.
"We can get the bus," Delph tells him.

The alphabet is missing from the bus too! All the letters are zooming off.

"How can we tell if it is the right bus or not?" groans Ralph.

"I think we need to run," sighs Delph. "We need to be quick!"

They see pamphlets on the road. Delph points at the pamphlets.
"The alphabet is still missing!"

They track the alphabet to Ralph's book club. Delph and Ralph creep up the steps.

They creep in and see Phillis the phantom. She looks mad.

Phillis the phantom runs the club. "Do you have a book for me, Ralph?" she booms.

"I lost it," mutters Ralph. "It was on my bed, but I lost it."

Just then, the letters of the alphabet land on Ralph's bag.

How odd, Ralph thinks. He tugs at the zip and peeks in the bag.

"My book!" yells Ralph. "How did it get there?"

Ralph gets the book from his bag and returns it to Phillis the phantom.

The alphabet zooms from Ralph's bag, to Phillis, and to the card in Delph's hand.

The alphabet letters land on the card.
"The alphabet is back!" yells Delph.

"Can you tell us what is on the card, Phillis?" begs Ralph.

"The book is in the bag. From Mum."
Delph and Ralph sigh.

The Alphabet Is Missing

1) What were Ralph and Delph looking for in Ralph's room?

2) What is the picture on the card of?
   a) A dolphin
   b) A tree
   c) A fish

3) Why do you think Phillis was angry?

4) Why do you think Mum moved Ralph's book?

5) Have you ever lost something? How did it make you feel?

©2022 **BookLife Publishing Ltd.**
King's Lynn, Norfolk PE30 4LS

ISBN 978-1-80155-068-0

All rights reserved. Printed in Poland.
A catalogue record for this book is available from the British Library.

The Alphabet Is Missing
Written by Madeline Tyler
Illustrated by Richard Bayley

An Introduction to BookLife Readers...

Our Readers have been specifically created in line with the London Institute of Education's approach to book banding and are phonetically decodable and ordered to support each phase of the Letters and Sounds document.

Each book has been created to provide the best possible reading and learning experience. Our aim is to share our love of books with children, providing both emerging readers and prolific page-turners with beautiful books that are guaranteed to provoke interest and learning, regardless of ability.

BOOK BAND GRADED using the Institute of Education's approach to levelling.

PHONETICALLY DECODABLE supporting each phase of Letters and Sounds.

EXERCISES AND QUESTIONS to offer reinforcement and to ascertain comprehension.

BEAUTIFULLY ILLUSTRATED to inspire and provoke engagement, providing a variety of styles for the reader to enjoy whilst reading through the series.

AUTHOR INSIGHT: MADELINE TYLER

Native to Norfolk, England, Madeline Tyler's intelligence and professionalism can be felt in the 50-plus books that she has written for BookLife Publishing. A graduate of Queen Mary University of London with a 1st Class degree in Comparative Literature, she also received a University Volunteering Award for helping children to read at a local school.

When she was a child, Madeline enjoyed playing the violin, and she now relaxes through yoga and reading books!

This book introduces the phoneme /ph/ and is a Blue+ Level 4+ book band.